The Little Flowers of Madame de Montespan

THE LITTLE FLOWERS of MADAME de MONTESPAN

JANE URQUHART

The Porcupine's Quill

Published by The Porcupine's Quill, Inc., Erin, Ontario
NOB 1TO. Financial assistance towards publication was received
from the Canada Council and the Ontario Arts Council.

Distributed by Firefly Books Ltd., 3520 Pharmacy Avenue,
Unit 1C, Scarborough, Ontario M1W 2T8.

Several of these poems have appeared previously in *Waves*.

Cover, and interior artwork, are from photographs by
Jennifer Dickson.

Executed at The Porcupine's Quill in December 1983.
Typeset in Sabon by Compeer (Toronto).

Edited for the press by Joe Rosenblatt, with Doris Cowan.

ISBN 0-88984-049-0

❀ This book is for Rikki and Guy.

The Baroque Bed

La Vallière, so 'tis said
Is losing favour fast
The King goes to her bed
With boredom unsurpassed

Now Montespan takes o'er
Things, as we've seen before
From hand to hand get passed

Eighteenth-century Street Song

SHADOW

The sun decides to
enter from the garden

moving on the carpet
he touches all your furniture
crawls under your closet door
investigates your wardrobe

moves his arms across
your memories
substituting light
heat and silence

he erases last year's
conversations with the stars
changes the contents of your mirrors
invents an alternative
palette for your crystal

scrapes his nails across brocade
revealing tangled threads
like contours on a map

he polishes your tables
his brilliance clings to cutlery
till spoons become large
bright incisions
all across the grain

a weight of gold and heat
he stops   burning
at the flesh of your neck

you are the only shadow in the room

The objects he had touched shifted. Walls crumbled. Courtiers vanished with crystal, cutlery and diamonds in their back pockets. Frescoes peeled. The garden grew.

II Absolute dispersal. There was, I'm told, a vast auction, which lasted for years. There was vandalism, forgery. And then the relocation, loose fragments drawn into new configurations.

III Catalogued items: a nail from the shoe of a horse. A broken mirror from a private chamber. A scrap of paper mapping out the garden. A cutting of brocade.

IV Saved artifacts: seven prayers he breathed in haste. Four denials. A goblet full of memories. An urn for everything forgotten.

V There, the display case exhibiting his women: passion, wit and reason. Sorrow, poison, order. Jewellery, costume and a broken quill pen.

VI Objects of pleasure: the prow of an imported golden gondola, the torn sail...a toy Spanish galleon. Fireworks, a miniature pageant, false porcelain from the first Trianon. Twelve masks, playing cards, dancing slippers. A stuffed swan.

VII The palace: gold leaf particles...a fractured fresco. This piece of marble, once part of a fountain. And then this candelabra, found not too long ago, intact.

THE ONE BEFORE

The one before
walked in these rooms
gazed in these mirrors
and searched her thighs for flaws

opening this cupboard
pouring this decanter
her mind set sail for landscapes
where you might stop
to choose a gift for her

a snowdrop pressed inside a book
birds frozen in a cage

the hours filled with
preservation of her flesh
her hair and face and muscle
till laying down her brush
she felt your absence speak

as though you hadn't nodded when
you passed her in the garden
or kept a place
beside you at the table

now I fill these rooms
and search the mirrors
I listen to the sound of strings
caressed by fountains

those imperfections in the glass
her face   thighs
lost in silver

the ghost travels with me
to your chamber

THE BAROQUE BED

From the framed centre
a cloth folds
its golden threads
brush the floor

brocade lambs graze
unicorns prance
a shepherdess in the shorn
world loses
her slipper in the chaos

white peacock
feathers at the edge
knots and tassels
dance in the air

they call this passion

I am lost in the fabric
smothered by your private furniture

I know the loom that dreamed this bed

GROTESQUE GEOMETRY

My dress conceals
the structure of the rooms

shaping afternoons into
a grotesque geometry

everything I touch
billows over edges

these sheets
                    those plumes
the satin skirt I fling aside

I appear in windows
I dissolve in doorways

outside my skin
your pulse is moving

growing through the silence
into confusion

BRIGHT RUMOURS

At night the window glass
reveals the self
the lamps cause fire

in the facets of my jewellery
and at my throat
bright rumours whisper

outside the garden turns away
and the windowpanes
reveal ourselves

outside
there is a gulf of darkness
where everything is watching

the other worlds have
vanished

in the morning
we're unable to see

Their Republic opened out towards the sea. Long fingers
extended to the lagoon. They returned by different routes in a
city like a maze.

II Here they sail over a false lake, a captive canal. Still waters
go nowhere. They encounter edges. Women won't call to them
from balconies. No one speaks of flowers...or the moon.

III And winter comes too soon. Skins bleach. Bones swell up
with dampness and the cold. Boats are frozen in a corner of
the garden.

IV They wish for raw confusion. Buildings that press back the
sun; bridges that teem with circumstances. Not the knives of
the doctors, bleeding winter diseases, the cold eyes of women
bored by the court.

V Sometimes at night they dream that their bloodstreams have
become canals, moving outwards, to the sea. Their lost city,
carried here inside the prison of their bodies.

VI They've forgotten the songs they used to sing.

1 Twelve candles
   and a dwarf

2 Costumes woven
   from garden leaves

3 Giant cogwheels
   motivating scenery

4 Gold slippers

5 Ribbons, ribbons

6 He is dressed in a hundred diamonds

7 Lights from memory: trap doors

8 A three-cornered hat with bells

9 Wild boars romp in a sea of flowers

10 Laughter

11 A solitary gesture

12 And my mask
    discarded

Artificial Fire

Des jeux de princes qui ne plaisent qu'a ceux qui les font.

Illustrative quotation from a dictionary

Protocol abandoned
he relaxes in the games room
he is fond and warm

and winning every time
a flicker of an eyelid
he gambles much
and loses little

while they listen for
the noise of
their coins in his pocket
he takes the scent of them
into his private rooms

their fingerprints on silver
he takes much of them
in the calm rooms
where the games are

he is fond and warm
winning every time

he leaves little of himself

the scent of them goes farther
they are
paying paying paying
for the favours of a king

WORDS

I've always had too much to say
the words
clever words   witty
they are shells from sovereign oceans
an eternal souvenir

words
pour them in the bodice
wear them
up and down the staircase

threading an amusing necklace
made of words
hear them click
together on the string

I'm spilling them behind my fan
I'm filling up my eyes
with necklace words

later there are silences
emptiness of rooms
he seldom visits

till the string breaks
and those words spill

like beads across a marble floor
in search of freer destinations

words

Never speak to women

unless you speak of flowers
illustrate the garden
and walk with them past fountains

but never let them carry your secrets
they are lapses
barricade the entrance
sing them songs

songs that have heat
put your head on ice
absorb their flesh
ride their passions
wear their fragrance
like a glove

give away nothing
unless it is disposable
fireworks at nightfall
gone from the sky
then gone from the memory
a cut flower
wilting on the stem

walk with them past fountains

don't tell your memories
they will follow
polish their flesh
till it shines
never make a trap of them

never speak to women
walk with them past fountains
fill their eyes with flowers

but never speak to them or
they will come to break you

You know the women

they have paused in your doorways
run their fingers over
your tapestries

memorized your garden

they have dressed for you
rearranged their features
their faces shine from mirrors

walking through the morning
on their thin ankles
blue veins glowing through
transparent skin
their nerves are humming
out to you

you turn your face away
you know the women

they have paused for
a moment in your doorways
while they are moving
dressed in transparent skins

I have a model, gleaming on my table. Cogwheels and cylinders, sharp and smooth. The machine is responsible for fountains. Moving water.

II Life in the garden.

III I found a larger model in a damp museum, housed in a case of glass and polished wood. Someone had entombed it, given it a brass plaque. I pushed a button and it began to move—even without fountains.

IV I told a friend in Paris that I like old clockworks. Disconnected from time...the predictable click of passing seconds, they become objects free of consequences.
    You should see the machine at Marly, he said.

V Someone had disconnected it, taken it away. Vanished.

VI In times of drought a hundred engineers worked the machine at Marly. They bent through the night over tables of rain. They interrupted rivers and creeks, sucked up lakes and ponds. The machine spread its system under the ground. It demanded the Seine, Loire, or Rhone.

VII A flicker of pleasure grew in the eyes of a king.

VIII In the autumn the north wind and the ghost of a machine at Marly.

IX How to dismantle such a machine? What to do with its parts?

x The garden is stripped of its surfaces. First I remove the fountains, then the statues, remove gravel and grasses and beds of low flowers. I roll up the brown earth. I expose the network of pipes leading to the Machine. Bones of the garden.

xi Pipes that lead nowhere.

xii In midsummer the machine becomes tired. I witness the fountains, long for the garden that it never saw, imagine labour. In his daily diary the King remarks that the fountains seem 'somewhat reluctant'.

xiii The Machine at Marly. Gone.

xiv It pushed and pumped. Everyone admired the fountains. Who admired the machine?

xv The heartbeat in my dream.

THE PALACE CLOSED

Yesterday your face shone
out beyond the gates
warm against my palm
its gold became a nugget

today
hard black iron
sharp enough to penetrate the sky
strong enough for denial
and the palace is closed

you mention vague repairs
religious holidays
your shadow travels
through the bars
filters through the windows
passes mirrors turning
darker than your heart

your shadow is locked
your palace is closed

I'm carrying
the glow of your face
here beside the fortune on my hand

vague repairs
religious holidays

patterns in the future
you've imposed upon my life

We were walking in the garden.

Several men with long tapes were measuring two statues—their height, their circumference. We paused to watch their labours.

They finished with one pair of marble figures, and after they had recorded their observations in small grey notebooks, they strolled away from us towards some other sculpture.

We followed. It began to rain. They juggled notebooks, tapes, and umbrellas. Their hands were red from working long hours out of doors. There was a combination of cinder and ink under their nails.

They saw us staring. The statues and the giant urns, they said, had somehow changed location in the last several years. They had been moved a few inches closer or a centimetre or so farther apart. The dimensions of some marbles had expanded while others had shrunk.

My friend pointed out that the palace never seemed to change as long as you stayed in the neighbourhood of the *tapis vert*; that it was always right there, at the top of the stairs, modest and comfortable and precisely the same size. No matter how far, no matter how close. He walked up and down to demonstrate with the palace in full view.

The workmen were clearly uninterested. They turned away, back to their tapes and notebooks. We left them and continued through the rain as far as the Grand Canal.

Later, it seemed that the statues had moved much farther apart but, as my friend said, *the palace stayed there at the top of the stairs*. Unconsciously we paced out the distance between one urn and the next. Passing the place where the men were working we waved to them and their hands fluttered.

We climbed the marble staircase. The hedges on either side opened up like curtains. Staggering, astonishingly huge, the palace emerged with wings and floors previously hidden. And still the space...continuously remote. The only way to lose that distance was to move around its massive edge and then away, always with our backs turned. Otherwise its giant image would follow us home.

We walked away. Deep inside the garden a measuring tape revealed the shrinking circumference of a marble thigh.

PLANET

You become the farthest planet

now I can't identify
these marks across your surface
lakes that might be shadows
craters turning dark
towards the sea

and still my notebooks
fill with your reversals
moments from this distance
I can barely understand

I am a prisoner of language
a prisoner of moments
no vehicles have been invented
to bring me any closer

each night the constellations
dance for my approval
the focus of my bent
inverted lens

while I am fixed on you
on moments I can barely understand

I am watching
taking notes

you are a circle of light
ten billion miles away

I am a prisoner of lenses
a prisoner of language

waiting for your bright
deceptive image to respond

NECESSARY PAUSE

A necessary pause
precedes the performance
just before dawn
splits open to morning

the hard morning pauses
they have held your shirt
caressed your stockings

pauses
moments turn back
those eyes that sweep
the crowd

they carry your relics
contemplate fountains

footsteps leave no traces
and the handwriting is burned

Kings have nightmares. Some dream of revolutionary mobs invading their private chambers...torches, knives. My King dreams of Terre Sauvage.

II   The Royal Gardener pauses. He unrolls a map of New France. Thin pencil lines reveal a garden plan. This pleases the King. He doffs his hat, mutters a few suggestions.

III   Miraculously, ships filled with hundreds of workmen arrive. The task of removing the giant primal forest begins. The first layer, undergrowth and bush, is removed. To the King's horror another layer of bush appears in seconds. Thicker than the first. No axe can penetrate its growth.

IV   Winter arrives, halting the project for ten months.

V   The following year Le Notre suggests they double the number of workmen and import trained French executioners to fell the trees. This pleases the King. He doffs his hat, re-examines the plan. He objects to the shapes of the decorative waters. They look like nothing more than a chain of great big lakes emptying into a canal, thin and irregular. Meaningless.

VI   Le Notre explains that they will make fine ice rinks for winter sports.

VII   The executioners have finally downed the trees. They begin sketching out allées and parterres upon the exposed earth. They begin digging and locate solid rock ten inches down.

VIII   Everything suddenly appears to change. The King finds himself alone, in a thick forest, his distance perception, sense of direction, completely addled. Light barely passes through the trees.

IX   Somewhere, vaguely to his left, there is a loud roaring noise, like wind. He stumbles through thorns and burrs in the direction of thunder. Bits of Royal brocade are left on branches.

X   He comes upon the waterfall. He is completely stunned. It lacks symmetry but none the less it is vaster than any waterwork he has ever seen. He wonders how Le Notre was able to design anything so powerful. He doffs his cerebral hat and imagines how greatly this will impress other monarchs. He decides to present Le Notre with a Dukedom.

XI   And then his foot slips on wet rocks. He plunges sceptre, robe and mantle into the churning rapids and flies over. He feels he has become the very centre of a fountain. SCREAMING.

XII   The following week he eliminates the word *glory* from his vocabulary.

BIRDS

He cannot make them stay
or stay out of the garden
they make their own decisions

he considers cages
giant aviaries
a mesh of metal among
the trees he has planted

some stay
others perch on the outside wire
they sing louder
disturb his morning sleep

the dogs of the hunt
whimper

some birds migrate farther south
they leave him looking for
their patterns in the sky

he desires the tiny hearts
of birds as jewellery
he invents special weapons to interrupt
their flight

generations later
their fragile eggs break
expose a path of grace notes
unharnessed by his will
it connects the garden

These are deceptive spaces

windows bronze
a cold stone warms

I'm trying to connect
the break in the horizon
moving distance after distance

there are canals
thin as gold leaf
and dreams of fountains
collapsing at the edge

trees that tremble
just beyond my hand
are miles and miles away
the oval mirror of the lake
impossible to reach

I am trying to move
distance after distance

turning back at dusk
my declaration of withdrawal

I see the garden
as near to me
and as far away

He chooses this location because there is no view.

II Here he can keep his personality intact. His lust tied.
   Directly in front of the palace there is a large hill. The small
immediate garden is enclosed on either side by steep cliffs.
There is little he can do. This is comforting, at least at first.
   He cannot live there. But he shall visit, and bring along his
favourites. He believes he will flourish in the company of
temporary intimacy and accessible green.

III He can't sleep. The cliffs cancel his dreams. There is a
pressure on the left and right sides of his brain. He is convinced
that the hill has moved closer. Twelve different engineers
measure the distance from his bed to the first incline of earth.
They assure him nothing has changed. He realizes this is
the problem.

IV He levels the hill.

V During his morning promenade the attending crowd is thin,
the atmosphere informal. They chat and giggle in his presence.
No one discusses glory or divine right, and the girls turn their
eyes to younger men.

VI He cuts into the cliffs, expands the castle. There is an army
draining the enormous outlying swamp. Soldiers in their
hundreds die of diseases connected to unhealthy soil. The
engineers bring water to the fountains at his palaces.

VII He builds four hundred fountains down through the vista
where the hill used to be.

VIII He dismantles, builds four hundred more.

IX Two thousand oak trees are brought in from the forests of the Jura. Half die in the process of transplantation. They are replaced with healthy giants. Well-ordered forests appear where once the cliffs used to be. But now they present a barrier to his view from the west and east rooms of the palace. A throbbing begins in his temples. The forests disappear. They are replaced by artificial lakes. Hundreds of guests float in imported gondolas.

X He demands and receives a large cascade where each of his mistresses are represented in stone as either goddesses or water nymphs. More forests appear where once there was only mud and toads. These he sees from his bedrooms, though they are five miles away!

XI He has broken the intimacy of rock and swamp wide open.

XII Now he feels much better.

XIII Sleep.

The Poisoned Shirt

A third chamber, as it were the anteroom of the above, is correctly named the decaying chamber . . . the walls are enormously thick.

Saint-Simon

The doctors come blindfolded
into the palace

they deliver babies
borne by masked women

anonymous screaming flesh

children
pulled from the womb
torn from the arms

the anonymous
flesh of the palace
taken to grow in
some other garden

next evening
the women perform at the ball
prepare their cards for the table

tiny fists
close up in their brains

Today I walked as far as the Trianons—an incredible distance. The garden around moves from one point to another. You do not pass it by like any other landscape. It crawls by you and the weather changes before it moves.

I walk away from the palace in a light drizzle, arriving at the Trianons with the sun full in the sky. It is broken into splinters on the west arm of the canal.

I arrive, realizing that there is very little of him left there. All that remains is one intimate allée, designed by Le Notre for a porcelain playhouse.

The whole geography has moved smoothly into another time.

And there is not a sign of me. The Trianon de Porcelaine is broken. I remain in a neutral room on the north side of the palace, fading into crowds of courtiers.

Walking back towards the palace I have to face the wind. It is almost dark.

The only thing I ever asked
was porcelain
a playhouse here
among the trees

you gave me faience
pretending to be porcelain

see the pools outside the door
blue and white
blue and white
convince me that is porcelain

porcelain and privacy
you gave me a forest of spyglasses
focusing on faience

blue and white
convince me this is porcelain

and permanence
unfolding here without
your strict approval
I want to keep
my small false castle
built within the time
frame of a miracle

the tiny garden with its urns
blue and white

you tear it down
because you cannot change it
improve it or expand it

the little structure
worked upon a lie

blue and white
blue and white
imaginary porcelain

shards sing
all around your feet

EVIDENCE

There were traces
there was evidence

the room moved in to
hold it
like a dark gold frame

we staggered round like saints
tiny ships sailed at our heels
lilies came to light

all evidence
the letter on the table
the ashes in the grate

until the day the dove
emerged

silent from your mouth

LE ROI S'AMUSE

The man who touches you
without love
arrives in a golden coach
drawn by a purebred horse

he carries his hands to you
like old sorrows

he is the death
of the child in you
the beginning of dark
there are no more songs
from the rooms
he moves through

the mouth he puts to yours
contains a brutal statement
your limbs become machinery
to the limits he enforces

he doesn't lure you into
altered landscapes
keeps his time in
artificial daylight
speaking solid words

and the last glimpse of
his sail on the horizon
never finishes

the stones that felt his step
the sea   the bed that you return to
all remember him

his breath remains
forever at your throat

remember him

Poison comes in phials filled with liquids, or packets filled with powders. It can be eaten, drunk, injected, or absorbed through the skin. Choose the scent. Often it is disguised as perfume.

II Madame de Montespan, not yet old, but fat from too many babies, registers extreme disapproval. The King is slinking secretly off to other beds. She wants to perfume the Venetian lace at his throat. She wants to powder his wig.

III No more aphrodisiacs. She administers them. He moves like a magnet to the iron charms of Madame de Fontagnes. She wants to sweeten that lady's tea, colour her eau de cologne.

IV *Arsenic, opium, antimony, hemlock.* Sitting alone in her rooms she shakes her head slightly. *Red sulphur, bat's blood, dried dust of moles, yellow sulphur.*

V Poison, a ritual extending from her body. The chalice rests on her stomach, her breasts fall away from her ribcage. It is the older woman, more wrinkled than herself. She whispers incantations and recipes into her ears. The younger one offers her flesh, like ripe fruit for the appetite of some darker power.

VI *Iron filings, resin of dried plums.*

VII She is falling, falling from favour. She hates him. She loves him. She sees him dead, surrounded by satin then safe in the tomb. *Her* poison trapped in his body like sperm in a uterus.

VIII During the ceremony she spells his name backwards on her inner thigh in donkey's blood. She spells his name forwards with some of her own. Someone saves the knife for a Baroque Forensic lab.

IX Decades later she pays four young women to remain in her room from nightfall to dawn. At her request they play cards and drink wine for ten dark hours. They laugh, gossip, while she hides behind the velvet curtains remembering the poison that perfumed her dreams.

X She thinks of the still, warm, dead heart of a pigeon, housed in a vermilion box, said to have power, but useless without the bird itself, without flight. Finally it had bloated, become putrid, had to be disposed of along with the box that held it.

XI Beyond the curtains the women discuss their lovers in the warm glow of the candles. Their smooth hands finger the cards nervously.

XII Madame de Montespan closes the lid on the poison.

In fields that unfurl to
the left of the garden
twelve grey horses
ease into canter

their loins adjust to
the three-beat rhythm

breaking like thunder
deep in the forest
flashing by branches
trampling moss

I never see them
here in this dream where
I'm pacing my limbs to
the nod of the trainer

here in this dream
educated muscle
covers the length of
my bones

I remember
clouds of rhythm
surrounding the palace

his step on the stair
his key in the lock

the supple behaviour

the hunt and the harness
unyielding

The poison is absorbed
into the meat of his back
the muscle

I want it to travel
nerves   sinews
chords of tissue
to answer the pluck of pain

I want to kill from without

the whole man
his body absorbing an entire
corruption

a final message from
blood to brain
until it bubbles away

the last sentence
frozen in his eyes

and me answering

Glass Coffins

It was not wise to leave so precious a relic in an undefended place outside the walls of town...because in those days a saint's body was esteemed more than a treasure.

The Little Flowers of Saint Clare

During this long winter we rarely go outside, though it is seldom warmer in our rooms. The interior of the palace has become a condensed winter world — cold mirrors, frozen chandeliers. Our fogged breath precedes us everywhere, softening candelabra and fresco.

It is as if the garden had completely disappeared. We can hear the wind and the groaning of the giant trees. But we never see outside. Thousands of window panes are covered by a thick frost.

There are no more gold settings at the table. Too much warmth in the cutlery is ridiculous. Soon the silver will disappear as well, reducing us to crockery.

It is February and we are surprised by a miraculous sun. He insists that we move outdoors, walk in his white garden. We don't object, put on our cloaks and boots, leave rooms for the first time in months.

At first we are overcome by endless snow and the shock of the first cold swallow of air, fresh on the tissues of our lungs. But when we can see again we are amazed by the unbroken surface of white and the open blue of the sky. The ground plan of the garden is erased by winter.

The statues are confused, awkward under hats and epaulets of snow. Urns grow ice. Our steps are new marks, making new boundaries.

We move towards the Bassin D'Apollon, watching as the metal forms take shape against white. We are able to pick the four horses, the sea monster, the torso of the young god emerging from his chariot. The wind has swept all the snow away from the Bassin, revealing enclosed ice, thick as marble. The sculpture is now locked, changed completely, made impotent by ice.

He, standing there looking at this, understands for the first time that all his monuments are immovable, frozen in their own time. They are like novelties on display, already under glass.

The Sun God and his Chariot, powerless in a cold, cold season.

The light, the wind, revealing all of this. Making the image totally clear. And totally brutal.

SILENCED

Autumn
false gold falling on actuality
stone walls all around

summer hid the prison
the perfect palace
draped in green and growing
overtop the stairs

winter now
and every word is opened
syllables ride to the horizon
in the grim hands of the post

false gold covers gravel
nothing hides in green

this palace
this prison

built in time
to silence
every loss I speak

LADY REASON

Emotionally
I am not yet ready for
Madame de Maintenon

Your Solidity
he calls her   or
Lady Reason

she answering
Majesty
Majesty

he bows
to the superior religion
she holds up a mirror to
his crime

his passion
the vanity of wars
and women won

landscapes pillaged

Lady Reason
Lady Reason
you move in a different realm

pulling out the power of
the lust of a King

his will to control
the world
himself

I am not ready for you

I am still
running through crooked
paths in my imagination

GLASS COFFINS

The women longed for glass coffins. They imagined that
centuries later men would file by to wonder at their incorrupt
flesh. They were also interested in satin pillows and narrow
couches. I know that this is true. One told me so herself.

II Glass coffins. Like the one the friars built around the body
of Saint Clare. Like the one that dwarfs placed Snow White in.
And these women *had* been kissed and kissed by their prince.

III Often the women chose their costumes for the sake of glass
coffins. They knew their fabric held together longest.

IV They arranged their hair in deathless styles.

V Between the covers, under the glass, their bodies shine.

We reason with one another, he prescribes the remedies, I omit
to take them and I recover. *Molière*

Doctor Fagon killed them all. I saw his window the other day,
filled with blades. Enormous scissors intersecting the rectangle.
And knives, knives.

II   Doctor Fagon enters the chamber in a brown cloak. He
bleeds the Queen. Laundresses delight in sheets stained
royally red.

III   Doctor Fagon performs his operations by the light of a
thousand candles. Muscles, soft to the scalpel, open over royal
bone. The silversmiths are busy building reliquaries all across
the country.

IV   *Earthworms against gout.*
     Bees' ashes to make hair grow.
     Ant oil against deafness.

V   Doctor Fagon senses hidden smallpox deep in the palace.
He administers emetics. Three princes vomit their way to
heaven. The iron heart of a King breaks open in the carriage
on the way to Marly.

VI Doctor Fagon mixes powders long into the night. He rebukes those that avoid him, accuses them of impiety. Museums prepare for his mortar and pestle.

VII He prepares for the King.

VIII Doctor Fagon broods over Burgundy wine. He doses the King with Spirit of Amber, rubs his left leg with hot cloths, wraps the royal limbs in linen soaked in brandy.

IX Eventually the pain evaporates. It leaves the palace by the back door, hovers somewhere east of the Grand Canal.

X Doctor Fagon cures the King. *The King is dead.*

Overhead the crystal hangs
handfuls of tears
in placid air

the mirrors divide
my body darkens
waiting in the hall

see me in the glass
reflected
see me in the glass
abandoned

I am walking back and forth
in a dream
never changing
my costume or my mind

I am blind
from staring too long at the sun

the scent of a King
is still in my hair

Photographs of Versailles* by JENNIFER DICKSON, R.A. courtesy of Wallack Art Editions, Ottawa. Jennifer Dickson works in collaboration with HOWARD WEINGARDEN in all technical aspects of the photographic processing and printing of her images.

COVER: 'Near the Grand Trianon'. Allée leading from the Grand Trianon, to infinity.

PAGE 2: 'Night, and the bird of darkness'. Parterre du Nord, Versailles.

PAGE 7: 'The French Pavilion'. Near the Petit Trianon, Versailles.

PAGE 17: 'Through the Crystal Wall'. Reflections of Mique's Belvedere; northwest gardens of the Petit Trianon, Versailles.

PAGE 39: 'Late afternoon: the Grand Trianon'. The Garden Drawing Room of the Grand Trianon, Versailles.

PAGE 53: 'Archway through the Queen's cabbagepatch'. Hameau de la Reine, Versailles.

*The artist gratefully acknowledges the financial assistance of the Canada Council, who funded her visit to Versailles in November, 1981.